Liberty

by Dona R. McDuff

Scott Foresman

Editorial Offices: Glenview, Illinois • New York, New York
Sales Offices: Reading, Massachusetts • Duluth, Georgia
Glenview, Illinois • Carrollton, Texas • Menlo Park, California

The date is October 28, 1886. The setting is New York City. Bands are playing. Guns are booming. Floats are moving slowly through the streets. Thousands of cheering people peer through the cold rain. They have come to see history in the making. President Cleveland is dedicating the Statue of Liberty.

But this event almost didn't take place. The years leading up to it were filled with many problems.

In 1865, in France, a group of friends had a dinner party. One of the guests thought it would be wonderful if France gave a gift to the United States for its hundredth birthday. It would be a symbol of freedom and independence.

A young artist was present at the dinner. His name was Bartholdi (Bar-TOHL-dee). He wanted to build statues that stood for the ideas he believed in. He thought a statue would be the perfect gift.

Bartholdi decided to visit America. On June 8, 1871, he set sail for New York. For thirteen stormy days at sea, Bartholdi tried to sketch the statue. Could he capture the feeling of freedom?

Some say that Bartholdi got the idea for his statue as soon as he arrived in New York Harbor. He saw a small island in the harbor. He knew this was the perfect site for his statue. Quickly he sketched a woman holding a torch. He called it *Liberty Enlightening the World.*

Bartholdi wanted to excite Americans about his idea. He also wanted them to share in the work. France would build the statue. America would build its base.

But he did not get much help at first. Many people thought the French should build the base. After all, the statue was supposed to be a gift from France.

Bartholdi did not give up. He returned home. After raising some money, he began the work. He started by making models for the statue. Each model was larger than the one before.

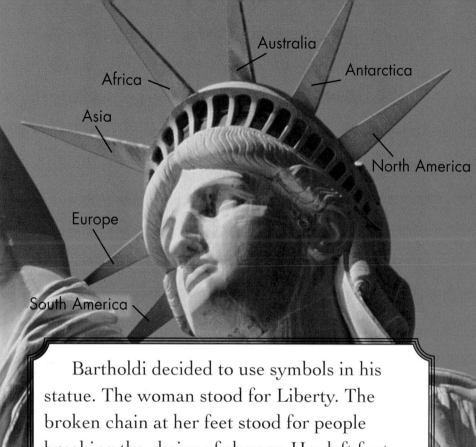

Australia

Antarctica

Africa

Asia

North America

Europe

South America

Bartholdi decided to use symbols in his statue. The woman stood for Liberty. The broken chain at her feet stood for people breaking the chains of slavery. Her left foot was placed forward to show that people were moving toward a new life.

The strongest symbol was the torch held in Liberty's right hand. The light would welcome new immigrants to America. In her left arm, Bartholdi placed a tablet that read July 4, 1776.

Liberty's crown had seven spikes. Each spike stood for a continent on Earth.

Bartholdi worked and worked on models
for his statue. The last model he made was
thirty-six feet tall. Now it was time to begin
the real statue. It would be four times as big!

Other artists helped. Using Bartholdi's
model, they took many measurements. The
finished model stood over 151 feet high.

Bartholdi knew that the statue could not be
built from stone. It would be much too heavy.
It would have a metal skeleton, covered with
copper skin.

Workers began by building huge wooden frames. They built one frame for each piece of the statue. Then the copper workers began their task. They hammered the thin copper sheets over the frames. Slowly the copper began to take on the shape of the statue. It took three hundred sheets of copper to cover the statue.

But something was needed to hold the copper statue together. A skeleton of steel belts would be built. The copper sheets would be attached to this skeleton. A famous engineer volunteered to do this job. His name was Eiffel (EYE-ful). He loved to solve tough scientific problems.

Bartholdi and Eiffel knew they could not finish the statue in time for America's birthday. So they decided to finish just the right arm and torch. They would send the arm and torch to the 1876 exhibition in Philadelphia.

At the exhibit people paid fifty cents to climb up into the hand and torch. The exhibit raised money for and interest in the project.

Another exhibit took place in 1878 in Paris. There, visitors to the World's Fair were able to view Liberty's head. Crowds stood in awe of its huge size.

Statue	Measurement
Chin to top of skull	17 ft., 3in.
Width of head (ear to eye)	10 ft.
Length of eye (corner to corner)	2 ft., 6 in.
Length of nose	4 ft., 6 in.
Width of mouth (corner to corner)	3 ft.

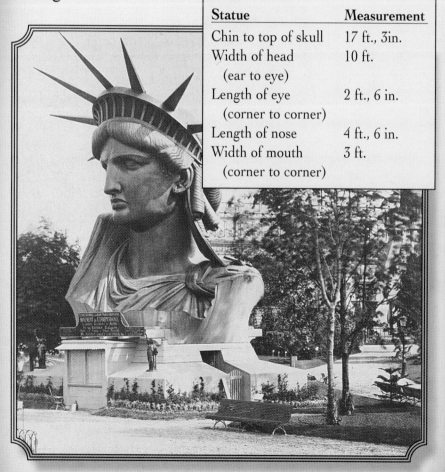

Liberty continued to grow taller. By June, 1884, she was dressed in her copper skin. She was ready to send to America.

But was America ready for Liberty? Bartholdi did not know that the Americans were having problems. A base had been built on Bedloe's Island. But no money was left to build the stone pedestal where the statue's feet would rest.

An American businessman helped to save the project. His name was Joseph Pulitzer. He was an immigrant. He knew the meaning of freedom and hope.

Pulitzer owned a newspaper called *The World*. He ran stories about the statue. He asked people to give money. The goal was to raise $100,000. He would print the names of all the donors as a thank you.

Many people gave to the fund. Even schoolchildren sent the few pennies they could. On August 11, 1885, *The World* printed the headline: ONE HUNDRED THOUSAND DOLLARS!

Work on the pedestal was finished in April, 1886. Some pennies, nickels, and dimes sent by people were placed around the last stone.

In Paris, Bartholdi's workers already had taken Liberty apart. They got her ready for her trip to America. It took 214 crates and seventy train cars to carry the statue to a ship!

The ship had to navigate its way across a stormy ocean. It took three weeks to reach New York.

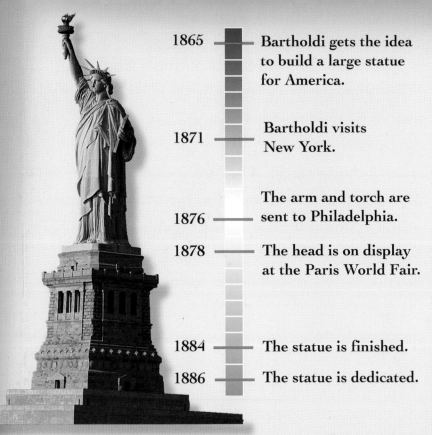

1865	Bartholdi gets the idea to build a large statue for America.
1871	Bartholdi visits New York.
1876	The arm and torch are sent to Philadelphia.
1878	The head is on display at the Paris World Fair.
1884	The statue is finished.
1886	The statue is dedicated.

At last, on October 28, 1886, America was set for the dedication. Bartholdi was high up inside the torch. A young boy on the ground was going to give him a signal when the last speaker finished. Then he would release the huge flag that covered Liberty's face

The speaker stopped to take a breath. The boy thought the speech was over and signaled Bartholdi. Bartholdi released the flag. The celebration began early!

For over a hundred years, the Statue of Liberty has stood in New York Harbor. Millions of immigrants got their first glimpse of America as their ships entered the harbor. These people had braved long, dangerous trips. Some had traveled through icy waters. These waters had chunks of ice that had broken off the northern glaciers. The statue promised hope to these weary newcomers.

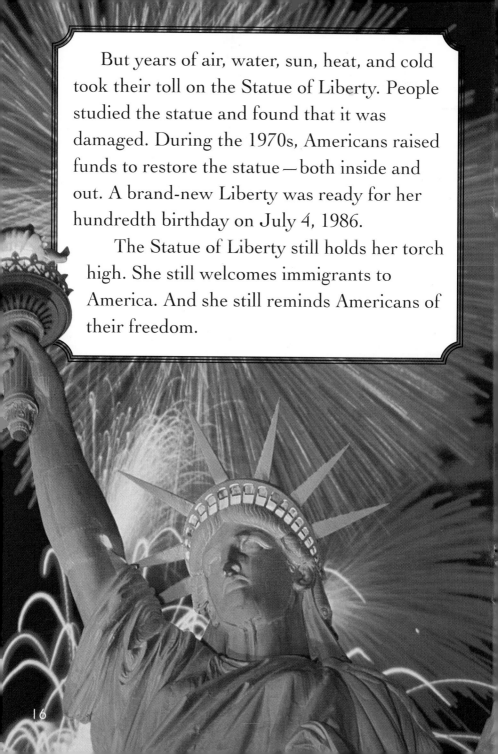

But years of air, water, sun, heat, and cold took their toll on the Statue of Liberty. People studied the statue and found that it was damaged. During the 1970s, Americans raised funds to restore the statue—both inside and out. A brand-new Liberty was ready for her hundredth birthday on July 4, 1986.

The Statue of Liberty still holds her torch high. She still welcomes immigrants to America. And she still reminds Americans of their freedom.